# FEELINGS

*by Leslie Carlisle*

Title: Feelings
Author: Leslie Carlisle
Copyright © 1995
First Edition, 1995
Second Printing, revised, 2012,
Published in the United States of America

# FOREWORD

Hey, Leslie! I thank God for blessing me with such a true friend, trusted confidant and "sister's keeper." You have been there for my family and me on countless occasions. I can never thank you enough for your precious friendship. God has given you many talents and gifts. Compassion, patience, and writing are just a few. I must also thank you for allowing me the privilege to take photos of you at the beach for your book cover. Most of all, I thank God for making it possible for you to write this inspirational book, which will encourage and uplift countless readers.

Congratulations, my friend,
Jackie McClain

## INSPIRATIONAL TESTIMONIAL

"The desire to consistently improve your life is one of your most fundamental needs. That feeling that comes from knowing that every day you can become better, have greater joy and live life more abundantly through Christ is an awesome gift. Regardless of where you've been or where you're going, you will find a body of useful information within the covers of this book. The reason is simple, we all have a story-a testimony to tell, the boldness to put pen to paper and expose ones life is an incredible and sometimes difficult task in itself.

I encourage you to read, digest and learn as you turn the pages. Meditate on what it is that God wants to reveal to you through the authors life experiences. They may give you some insight into your own life. Be Blessed"

~Pastor Alonzo Morris

# Feelings

BLACK CHILD..................................................................6
COME CLOSER TEACHER ...................................................7
DREAMS UNLOCKED..........................................................9
"FEELINGS" ...................................................................11
GIRLFRIEND.................................................................12
HURTING TIMES..............................................................14
I'M SINGLE...................................................................15
I KNOW........................................................................16
JESUS ANSWERS .............................................................17
JESUS ANSWERS; THE EPILOGUE....................................18
LEAVING YOU ................................................................20
LOST............................................................................22
MAGICAL LAND...............................................................24
NO LONGER HERE ...........................................................25
RETREATS OF ONES LIFE .................................................26
SEE THE OTHER GREEN ...................................................30
THE BABY SHOWER..........................................................31
THE PULPIT AWAITS YOU ................................................32
TIMEKEEPER..................................................................34
WATCHING YOU ..............................................................36
MANY THANK-YOUS .........................................................38

## BLACK CHILD

*Who is this black child in the mirror?*
*With curly hair braids, corn rows, pigtails and*
*nappy hair.*
*Who is this black child, with many shades of*
*color?*
*Black like midnight, brown like honey wheat,*
*tan like the African sands.*
*Who is this black child?*
*Jumping rope with the double dutch beat with*
*fancy stepping feet.*
*Having fun with the children on the street.*
*Who is this black child?*
*Learning shapes, numbers, letter, and colors.*
*Finding out the importance of sharing and*
*getting along with others*
*In order to become all that this child can*
*become.*
*Who is this black child?*
*With a vision, insight, dreams, hope and love to*
*give and to receive.*
*Who is this black child?*
*This black child is the child of the future.*

# COME CLOSER TEACHER

*Tell me something teacher that I really want to know.*
*Why can't you come closer, so I can tell you what I know?*
*How can I learn from you, when you sit so far from me?*
*Yea, hand me some cut out shapes and colors and a little dap of the past.*
*You tell me what you want me to do.*
*Where to put this and where to put that.*
*You hurry me on, not giving me the time to create all that I can.*
*That which is within my hands and mind.*
*Tell me something teacher that I really want to know.*
*Why can't you come closer so I can show you what I know?*
*Then that way if I make a mistake, as I often do you'll be right there beside me to redirect my steps.*
*You won't be sitting on the porch or fixing coffee at the sink.*
*You won't be reading up on the morning news from the other side of the room.*
*For all that seems so far from me.*
*Tell me something teacher that I really want to know.*
*Why can't you come closer so that I can show you what I know?*
*When you sit so far away there are special things that you will miss.*

*So come a little closer teacher and see my world with me.*

## DREAMS UNLOCKED

*My life with all its expressions and emotions
have been sitting upon the shelf
all locked up, for many years.
Not knowing how to say what was all inside of
me to say
like the butterfly when it's in the cocoon stage
right before it breaks out of the little hole
locked inside with not enough room to move
around
to breath fresh air or to express itself.
My life with all it's expression and emotional
writing plans
dreams and visions of this writer resembles the
cocoon.
Sitting on the shelf collecting dust day after day,
week after week, month after month
locked up so tightly
out of sight from the world to see and hear
to enjoy, to be encouraged, enlightened from my
mind.
All because of a lack of confidence, of mounting
excuses
not enough strength to take yet another step
forward
obstacles in my way
losing sight of the vision almost forgetting about
the dreams
in the procrastination!
What now?
Do I give up?
Quit and become a failure?*

*Walk away from all my dreams, visions and hopes*
*that I have for me and others?*
*My life with all its expressions and emotions*
*have been sitting upon the shelf of life*
*all locked up for many years*
*written plans, dreams and visions of this writer*
*I must not quit though; I know I have to go on.*
*For nobody can express my writings and visions*
*but me.*
*I must share the insight that I feel.*
*For I must go on.*
*For I must not lose sight of my dreams of my visions.*
*And failure is not an option...*

## "FEELINGS"

*something deep within my soul*
*way down deep inside of me.*
*Something that just won't let me be.*
*Oh, it stirs me now and then*
*almost taking me for a spin.*
*For it starts from my beginnings*
*up to this very day.*
*Oh, I have feelings and*
*I must express from deep inside of me.*
*For they surface over and over as they flow out*
*of me.*
*You don't know when they will start*
*and where they will end.*
*All you know is that they are feelings.*
*Something from within.*

## GIRLFRIEND

*GIRLFRIEND,*
*oh what a special name to have*
*for it means so very much to me.*
*It isn't just a passing word.*
*It's meaning has roots that grow.*
*It means I really know you*
*and you know me.*
*And our lives have touched*
*we have shared a special closeness.*
*That nobody has shared.*

*GIRLFRIEND*
*we have been there for each other*
*through hurt, pain and despair.*
*Happy times*
*sad times,*
*rocky times,*
*joyful times*
*and we made it through.*

*GIRLFRIEND,*

*you have listened to me,*
*I have listened to you*
*as we each poured out our life's stories.*
*We let each other talk it out*
*we waited for time to pass*
*when It was time to say something*
*to encourage and up lift each other's heart.*
*So I stop once again to let you know*
*that you mean much to me.*

GIRLFRIEND,

*Oh what a special name to have*
*for it means so very much to me.*
*It isn't just a passing word.*
*It's meaning has roots that grow.*
*Thank you for all the special times*
*that we have shared.*
*Thank you for caring and sharing,*
*laughing and crying*
*and for our lives touching*
*like only true girlfriends can do.*

## HURTING TIMES

*people ask me how I feel*
*and my answer is always,*
*"fine, thank you."*
*as they walk away*
*I glance toward their direction*
*and ask myself*
*do they know how much I hurt?*
*Can they see my puffy eyes?*
*Can they feel my hurting heart?*
*As they gently walk on by*
*people ask me about the makeup I wear*
*the color and the shades that I use*
*for they would like to try them too*
*I want to say real loud some days*
*that it's just a mask to hide the blues inside of me*
*this happy made-up face is breaking*
*you just can't see the pain that I'm erasing.*

## I'M SINGLE

who am I?
I am somebody special.
A mother, father, sister, brother, aunt or uncle.
But I'm single.

Who am I?
I am a child of the king.
A chosen vessel for him to use in the ministry.
A child on a journey to the Promised Land.
But I'm single.

Who am I?
Your brother or your sister in Christ.
Your neighbor, friend, coworker prayer partner.
But I'm single

who am I?
A child of the king with similar struggles, trials
and tribulations.
Good days, bad days, happy and sad days turned
upside down

who am I?
I am somebody special.
Won't you take the time to know of me.
For I have a special personality
just like you I am special too.
Who am I?
I'm single,
but not alone...

## I KNOW

you are searching
looking for the glamour
the lights
the stars
the cars
and the fast money.

I KNOW
you want to drive the shiniest
and longest car
drink the latest drinks
and wear the latest fashions

I KNOW
you're looking for quick money
fast highs
all to travel in the fast lane?

I KNOW
also a friend that holds the light
and stars in his hand
a friend that can change
your sad into glad.
A friend whose name
is the only name to call upon

I KNOW
he will answer every call
and his name is
JESUS

# JESUS ANSWERS

*Jesus said one day, "would you take a walk with me?"*
*without hesitation I said "yes."*
*while we were walking, he said, "though me you may not see,*
*I am here right by your side.*
*I'll be there when the clouds hand low, blinding you so you can't find your way.*
*Or when storms of life seem to strong for you to face.*
*You will have to continue on your way with me and a prayer*
*for my father answers prayers.*
*When life gives you a wrong turn and a bumpier road,*
*I will walk that road with you.*
*I will never leave you.*
*For my love is everlasting.*
*I will keep walking with you all along life's way.*
*When tears weigh you down and you lose a little self-control,*
*and the inner pain you can't bear anymore,*
*I will guide you with the Holy Spirit.*
*I will keep walking with you.*
*When the clouds roll away and one of many storms are gone for now*
*and your cheeks are dry from the tears, I will keep walking with you.*
*I will never leave you.*
*You begin to notice the sun is shining again and the rainbows that swing across the sky's,*

*untouched.*
*As the inner pain begins to fade and you are*
*feeling whole again, at my side,*
*you should know in your heart of hearts that I*
*had been there*
*and will always walk with you.*
*So you just keep on moving,*
*walk on, you are not alone.*

## JESUS ANSWERS; THE EPILOGUE

*do you remember that day you asked me if I*
*would come and take a walk with you?*
*And without any question or hesitation, I said*
*yes.*
*I want you to know that with your love*
*I am still walking and believing and I know you*
*are still here right by my side*
*I will keep on walking with you; my faith*
*strengthening with every step.*
*When clouds are hanging so low that they blind*
*me until I can't see my way*
*when the storms of life are too strong for me to*
*weather.*
*I know that I will just have to pray and go on.*
*As life drives me through the wrong turns and*
*down many a bumpy road*
*we will just walk it together.*
*I will keep on walking with you, trusting you*
*with every step.*
*When tears weigh me down and I lose a little*
*self-control*
*with the inner pain I think I can't bear;*

*when the clouds rolls away and one of many*
*storms are gone for now*
*my cheeks being dry from tears*
*I will keep walking with you, in faith, I will keep*
*walking with you.*

## LEAVING YOU

it was hard this time, leaving you, walking
away.
Why didn't I say it; why did I wait?
It might be too late to express what was on my
mind and in my heart.
You had been right there sitting next to me and
I couldn't express it to you,
all that I was feeling and all the things that I
wanted to say.
The magical vibes I was receiving
the words got lost
maybe it wasn't the right time, if there is a
wrong and right time.
I am a toucher and I wanted to hold your hand
I wanted to touch your cheek and glance into
your eyes
I wanted to hold you and rest in the peace of the
moment.
Why didn't I say it out loud to you once and for
all, that I cared.
I mean I really care and you mean a lot to me.
And I really don't want to leave you right now.
I wanted to stop, I wanted to talk some more.
Just hold your hand.
Wanted to walk side by side and share special
moments.
Don't send me away before we express this
moment in this special time.
The words need to come, they need to be said, the
vibes need to be answered, before I board the
plane.

*Don't send me off to drift into the clouds to get
lost in the darkness of the heavens.
Reach out to me don't let me leave. Take me into
your arms and hold me, let me stay.
Even if it's just for one more day.
Leaving you sounds so permanent and final.
Leaving you feels sad and empty.
Please don't let me go don't let me leave you,
for I really want to stay.*

# LOST

*locked up in a hotel room in Salt Lake City*
*thousands of miles from home.*
*Away from the world I knew and people I loved.*
*Depression drowning my body, overtaking my*
*mind.*
*Where Nobody knew where I was and I really*
*didn't care at the time.*
*I was just there.*
*Sitting at the desk looking out the window, going*
*back over my life.*
*Seeing no hope out from this lonely pain.*
*I just couldn't go on cause I would be insane.*
*Counting the pills in my hand and on the*
*desktop I just knew I would soon have rest*
*a lot of peaceful rest.*
*My mind tired and body stressed, all my*
*strength almost gone.*
*I bowed my head closed my eyes prayed to Jesus*
*for one more last time.*
*I just let Jesus know how tired and lonely I was.*
*I asked for new direction and faith.*
*And courage so I could run in this Christian*
*race.*
*I don't remember when I fell asleep.*
*Did I finish praying?*
*Was my prayer long enough?*
*I do know one thing for sure, Jesus answers*
*prayer.*
*For I awoke to brand new day.*
*Full of hope and the promises Jesus gave.*
*Pills untouched and out of the way.*

*Now I can begin my day.*

## MAGICAL LAND

*I was a child of nine years old*
*with long black braids, ribbons and bows.*

*I was a child of nine years old*
*with magical dreams and a runny nose.*

*A very sickly nine year old.*
*This nine year old child*
*had the company of the most magical shape-able,*
*moveable, talkative, dramatic, expensive,*
*perfume bottles you could dream of.*

*I was a child of nine years old*
*with a stage of bottles*
*with many places to go.*

*We marched to the beat of clapping hands*
*we ran around with scarves in our hands*
*we had lunch together and fell asleep.*
*We woke up again with a brand new beat*
*in magical land.*

*Yes, I was a child of nine years old*
*with long black braids, ribbons, and bows.*

## NO LONGER HERE

when I have gone out from this life
please don't be sad when you think of me.

When you see rainbows full of God's promises
you'll smile knowing how much I loved the
rainbows.

When you see young children playing
think of how many I have helped and cared for
them,
loved and nurtured them
when they were in my care.

As you walk among beaches,
sand under foot
you will be reminded of me
and my love for the peace and strength
that I had always gathered from the beaches
oceans, sand and sea.
Then your heart will be warmed.

When I have gone out from this life
please don't be sad when you think of me.

While you gather together to say your good byes,
don't be sad, hold your head high,
and keep your hands in God's unchanging hands,
and walk on through his life.

Walk on, for I will be no longer here.

## RETREATS OF ONES LIFE

*You say what are retreats?*
*What does it mean?*
*Is it good for me?*
*Then I say where do I start?*
*How can I explain?*
*So that you may understand*
*then you and I*
*can take care of that inner man.*

*Doctor, nurses*
*lawyers judges,*
*preachers, teachers*
*and people reaching out,*
*lend me your ears*
*and open your heart*
*we are in for a brand new start.*

*You must be able to pray*
*then listen to your heart*
*as the Lord's answer comes*
*whispering*
*and giving you*
*and I a second start.*

*When listening to the Lord*
*he will answer you*
*he'll restore, refill,*
*rebuild, encourage,*
*uplift, motivate*
*and move you up to higher heights.*

*He'll open doors*
*while closing others,*
*heal you from the inside out,*
*guide and direct you,*
*and will never leave you alone.*
*It all starts with the retreats,*
*in one's life.*
*You say what are retreats?*
*What does it mean?*
*Is it good for you?*

*It means to relax off to yourself,*
*getting away to escape.*
*Whether it's lunch all by yourself,*
*airplane ride,*
*walks on the beach*
*to see footprints in the sand.*
*It's a personal conversation*
*between you and the lord. It can be in town*
*out of town*
*around and downtown*
*as long as you get away to yourself.*
*Doctors, nurses,*
*lawyers, judges,*
*preachers, teachers*
*for people reaching out.*

*You who advise,*
*counsel.*
*Research*
*chart history.*
*Those who are called upon each day to*
*listen,*
*pray,*

*explain life,*
*encourage,*
*nurture,*
*hug, redirect,*
*restore*
*life back to wholeness*
*by the aide of the holy spirit.*
*It's an emptying out of oneself*
*sharing and giving*
*to another human being.*
*Then your own self need to be*
*refilled,*
*restored.*
*This is when you retreat.*
*Walk away for a day.*
*Find shelter for the hurting times.*
*In all your retreats*
*never let go of God's unchanging hand.*
*For he will carry you through*
*bring you out of the storm.*
*So when you find yourself in the midst of a*
*storm,*
*hold your head high*
*and walk through the storm.*
*Let the Lord be your refuge.*
*Your shelter,*
*your hiding place*
*your rock*
*your all in all*
*you say what are retreats?*
*What does it mean?*
*Is it good for me?*
*Yes good for you and me.*

*Not every day, but now and then we need
retreats in our lives.
May you have many and share the retreats in
your life.
With others so they can begin their retreats.*

## SEE THE OTHER GREEN

*I see the green that others see*
*The signal light,*
*Grass, apples and trees*
*String beans*
*Kool Aid*
*Cabbage and greens*
*I see the green that others see*
*That frightens me*
*Money... money... money...*
*Greed... greed... greed...*
*The famous paper faces of*
*Washington, Lincoln, Jefferson and Grant.*
*This is the green that frightens me.*
*This is the green that frightens me*
*For it breaks up, tears down and destroys the*
*families*
*Kills, steals, robs our children's destiny.*
*Green should be a sign of growth*
*Strength*
*Unity*
*And love*
*Among our folks.*
*This and only this is the other green to me.*

# THE BABY SHOWER

*Gathering of friends and relatives all walking in*
*on time*
*Greeting each other with hugs and kisses*
*Signs of affection and love*
*As I look around I see the different shapes and*
*sizes*
*The balloons with all the colors of the rainbow*
*Mountains of gifts for this new bundle of joy*
*Before he or she takes the first step or holds the*
*first bottle or utter first words*
*This child's history of family and friends begin a*
*lifetime journey*
*The sounds I hear are happy, joyful laughter*
*Each gift so special and unique*
*Only means each person took time alone with*
*effort*
*Had to be the right size, color and shape for this*
*little bundle of joy*
*Pictures were taken of this special day*
*So he or she can have a lifetime of memories*
*that started today*
*The show is over; the cake is all gone*
*Gifts are put away 'til this child is born*
*As the day comes to an end, friends and*
*relatives depart*
*With more hugs and a few more kisses*
*They take with them the joy of this event in*
*their hearts*

## THE PULPIT AWAITS YOU

*The Master has called you through the Holy
Spirit
The time is now
For the pulpit awaits you.
I know you prayed many a prayer
You have sung many a hymn
You have served many people while leading
them to the master
Your mission has not yet come to an end
For the pulpit awaits you.
Oh what a special time in your life and the life
of your family and friend to celebrate the
richness
And goodness of the masters handiwork
For he has brought you a mighty long ways and
he's not finished yet
For the pulpit awaits you
Through dark and troubled days and nights,
when you didn't know your way
Lonely nights filled with disappointment and
despair
Through trials and tribulations, you stood
steadfast in your master's care
You have kept your hand in the master's
unchanging hands and he has carried you
through
You have been in many storms, but you have
weathered each one of them
Now the pulpit awaits you
Oh, I hear your soft unspoken questions
Will there be more trials and tribulations?*

*Are all the storm clouds gone?*
*Will it be smooth sailing from this point on?*
*Oh, I think you know the answer*
*For this is when Satan will come to you in any*
*way, shape, form or fashion.*
*He will test you, tempt you and throw you a*
*curve or two*
*Shake you and try his best to break you any*
*way he can*
*Still the pulpit awaits you*
*Take a tighter hold to the master's unchanging*
*hands, for you'll need humbleness, prayer*
*Patience, faith and plenty of rest*
*Cause you'll be up against Satan at his very best.*
*But the pulpit awaits you*
*Long sleepless nights of studying God's word*
*Phone calls in the middle of the night. Meetings*
*and hospital visits*
*More trials and tribulations,*
*Struggles, pain and heartaches, a few storm*
*clouds*
*The master knows your heart, and he has heard*
*your prayers for he is the potter and you are the*
*clay*
*Yes, the Master has called you through the Holy*
*Spirit. The time is now*
*For the pulpit awaits*

## TIMEKEEPER

*Timekeeper, timekeeper*
*It's time to stop keeping time*
*It's time to join other circles*
*Plan tea parties*
*Go to luncheons*
*Sit down with new friends like these*
*Timekeeper, timekeeper*
*It's time to stop keeping time*
*It's time to walk along your master's beaches*
*And place your footprints in the sands of time*
*And listen to your master's voice*
*As he whispers peace be still.*
*Timekeeper, timekeeper*
*It's time to stop keeping time*
*It's time to spend more time traveling*
*And spreading your master's word.*
*To stop and smell the flowers*
*Their fragrance soft and sweet*
*To touch more lives*
*In your own special way*
*Like you have touched ours*
*Timekeeper, timekeeper*
*It's time to stop keeping time*
*We're here tonight*
*To thank you for the time*
*You have spent with us*
*We thank you for your tears*
*Laughter, hugs, patience*
*Wisdom, foresight*
*We will treasure all of them*
*And keep them in our hearts.*

*But timekeeper, timekeeper*
*It's time to stop keeping time.*

## WATCHING YOU

*I was watching you*
*And what you showed me*
*Will stay with me*
*Not just this day*
*But forever*
*You showed me that the family*
*Was a very important unit*
*And that a parent can be a mother or father*

*I was watching you being a father*
*Taking care of your children.*
*Making sure that they were all right.*
*A wonderful father, brother, cousin, nephew,*
*That made me proud of you*

*I was watching you*
*And you showed me*
*The love*
*Nurturing*
*Understanding*
*Determination*
*Sacrifices*
*It took to be a parent*
*And now as a parent myself*
*When I say "No"*
*I won't help you anymore*

*Then I remember what I saw in you*
*While I was watching you*
*Then I to became more understanding*
*I nurtured a little more*

I go an extra mile
Because somebodies watching me
Like I watched you
You wanted us to remember
The days of long ago...
And the present...

So you took pictures
As we gathered for celebrations
As a family
And today we gather
For yet another family celebration
You're home-going to the promise land
We love you
We thank you
For being in our family
On this day we began to take the pictures
Love and nurture our families
With understanding and love.
For now you are watching us...
For now you are watching us...

## MANY THANK-YOUS

*First and foremost I want to thank Jesus for being my friend! For he has always been there for me even when I walked or ran away from him, wanting to do my own thing, in my own time. Jesus stayed right at my side, he never left me. He promised that he would never leave me alone. Jesus is a promise-keeper.*

*Then I would like to thank my family for our closeness, love and encouragement that we give each other. For that is what makes us a family.*

*To all the special people that have touched my life along the way. I thank you. I can't and won't name you one by one in fear that I will leave someone out. Like when I was back east almost homeless and this older couple bought me a winter coat and just left. But I wore their love all winter long and other winters that came. I can't leave them out. The subway driver that I wouldn't go home with. I had to stay on the subway for three days and two nights homeless by my own choosing. He would bring me big lunches in the morning to last all day money to ride the subway and go to the movies, the warm rich pair of winter boots. He just would make sure I was all right. He told the other drivers to keep an eye on me. I call them unknown heroes.*

*All through my life Jesus has sent his chosen vessels to watch over me. Some have names others don't and they are just as important. I thank each and every one of them. To all that have touched a part of my life, that means if we have held hands hugged, cried together, spent time together, That time I thank you for. May God bless you each day.*

*Thanks to all my past and present pastors and deacons that gave me spiritual food all my life. Thanks to my Teachers and co-workers in the field of child development. I find it a joy to be among educators for young creative minds. To my mentors past and present that have taught, guided and showed me a better way.*

*To past and present staff, teachers and classmates in the field of Christian education. Because of that special time together and what we all learned from God's word we will never be that same. Thank you from my heart of hearts to past and present church families. Thank you for letting me experience the joy of having more than one family. Again, I thank everyone for being a part of my life. I would like to take this time to thank those who will be reading my first writings. I hope I have said something to each one of you through my writings that will encourage, uplift and move you. And I'd like to add a special thank you to all those who encouraged and critiqued my work in my literary family, Zica! Also, last but not least, many special thanks to my first editor and friend, Loretta; who from beginning to end has been there for me. We've accomplished a lot together, girl!*

*Thank you.*
*~Leslie*

## TO MY DAUGHTER

When my daughter told me to write a foreword, I really didn't know how to start. She has been into so many things. As a child, I recall her playing in my bedroom with my perfume bottles. She would sit there for hours at a time, each and every day, picking the bottles up, arranging and admiring them. She spoke to them as if they were her pupils. I guess in the back of her mind, she knew she would be a teacher, and the bottles were instrumental in forming that thought.

As she grew older, she became more involved in Sunday school and church activities. She was only about eleven or twelve years old when she began helping teach the children. Her dad was a Baptist, and I, her mother, a Methodist. She attended both churches, at different times, working with the children and singing in the choir. As a teen-aged, school student, Leslie still found time to teach others. And I must say, she still found time to enjoy my perfume bottles.

Leslie kept active in many, many things, especially the church. Before I knew it, she was off to college, studying child development, and making plans to teach. Now, I'm proud to say, she's a Teacher in the Sacramento City Unified School District's Children's Centers.

This, her first book, is evidence of her FEELINGS about God, life and love. Leslie is the child I bore, (but a child no more) and is my greatest love of all. She's a caring, selfless, *thoughtful, and creative human being, who I am proud to call my child.*

## MESSAGE TO MY MOM

Mom, I hope this message brings joy to your day along with a smile to brighten your world like you have brightened mine. I couldn't bring this, my first book, to a close without a message to you, for you have always been a very special part of my life.

First of all, thank you for being my Mom!

Thank you for all the encouragement and love you have given me during my life.

Thank you for being my listening post as you listened to me talk and read my poems for my book.

Thank you for being truthful with your feedback about my work.

Thank you for always being there for me in good times and in bad times.

Thank you, Mom for calling things right when they were both right and wrong. Especially things went wrong.

Thanks for giving direction, insight, wisdom, humor and most of all for sharing your love and trust in Jesus Christ.

In closing, I just want to say, from my heart to yours, I love you, respect you, admire you and am very proud of you. I'm glad you are my Mom. May God bless you, not just this day but always.

Love you!
Your daughter,
~Leslie~
In remembrance of Inez Carlisle—1913 - 1995

## TO DAD WITH LOVE

*I think of you often since passed away some eighteen years ago. It always seems like just yesterday that I had you in my life as my father and mentor. You shared with me and countless others your humbleness, gentleness, love, understanding, patience, wisdom, insight and most of all your love for Jesus.*

*All anybody had to do was start talking about their problems and you would tell them how Jesus could love them. I recall how you would gather me up each Sunday morning and take me to Sunday school. That was part of the foundation you gave your family. That love will last longer than time itself. It's sure to be passed down through generations to come. You always wanted me to be a part of the church family; to get involved and interact with the church.*

*And in doing so, I would also learn more about interacting positively with my family, elders, teachers, and friends. I quietly listened and took in as much or the sermons I could. A lot of the lessons I kept stored away for a later time. Things that were said would come back to me at different times in my life. Listening is important. Saying "thank you" and sharing what you had freely with others came so easy to you. Upon entering a room you would always say "hello," or something else uplifting, reminding me that it was my job to do the same. I miss you, Dad, especially when I'm going through something really rough. Thanks to you, I have a guidebook that you directed me to a* long time ago; that's God's holy word. I found that when planted in your heart, God's holy word would give your life meaning, peace, joy, love, patience, humbleness, direction and so much more.

You wanted so much for me to slow down in my life. Do more changing, take life more serious. I didn't' do all that before you left me. I made a lot of U-Turns, but thanks to you I found my way back to Jesus. I learned that if you keep your hands in God's hands, he would never leave you alone. I look around at the men and women in our family, and I can see you somewhere in all of them. When I close my eyes long enough I can see you. Your smile, your walk, and that gentle conversation. I love you so much. When I want to remember how much others loved you, all I have to do is close my eyes and remember the day of your funeral when we were en route to the graveside. Someone told me as we turned the corner, to look back and see all the lights. For as long as you could see, countless numbers followed us. That imagery gives me comfort and peace even today. So many loved you.

Thank you, Dad for all the love you filled my life with. Thank you for the wonderful childhood and for telling me about your friend, Jesus. For you gave me the right foundation to be able to move through this life. Through hard times and good times, I will keep my hands in God's unchanging hands. He and only he can see me through.

www.ingramcontent.com/pod-product-compliance
Lightning Source LLC
Chambersburg PA
CBHW071749020426
42331CB00008B/2233